Also by Niall Bourke

Line (Tramp Press, 2021)

Did you Put the Weasels Out? (Eyewear, 2018)

THE ERECTION SPECIALIST

Bourke

The author expressses his sincere thanks to Arts Council England whose generous funding made this collection possible.

ISBN: 978-1-915079-07-7

Cover designed by Aaron Kent

Edited and typeset by Aaron Kent

Broken Sleep Books Ltd
Rhydwen,
Talgarreg,
SA44 4HB
Wales

Supported using public funding by
ARTS COUNCIL ENGLAND

LOTTERY FUNDED

Contents

The Erection Specialist

Niall Bourke

A thick-necked prick from Gort wants you to help him put up a tent somewhere out the back-arse of Letterfrack.

Will you go with him? And will you survive if you do?

Only YOU get to decide!

The Erection Specialist 1

Half-fucking-six he picks you up
in the end. Half-fucking-six,
after telling you to be in Salthill for half-five,

when you'd called him the day before,
rang the number in The Advertiser:
Erection Specialist Needed

(well now that'd got your attention –
labourers to put up a marquee)

where in Salthill? you'd asked him,
the bit near the sea, he'd said and then hung up.
The bit near the sea.
The bit near the fucking sea.
Ah he'd sicken your hole,
and sure you should've known then.

So there you are, you and a young lad

(Murtagh his name was, you find out,
in the end,
when you read it
in the paper)

and waiting for nearly an hour,
walking laps of a flicketing streetlamp
circling it like a pair a bicycles afraid
ye'll tip over if you stop,

stamping your feet awake in your boots,
blowing billows of breath into cupped-up
hands and dreaming of being buried
back in your beds, but quiet though,
not much chat that hour of the morning,
ye can both tell it's shaping up to be a cunt
of a day, something about it,
the grawness of it maybe,

and you're only ayting through the fags,
one then the other then the other,
nom nom nom
nearly quarter of the box gone
when the sour prick finally screeches
up in the van

(a brand-new Mercedes Sprinter mind,
ah he had no problem spending money
on the van, he looked after that right enough)

and he rolls down the window
and you see his big slab of a head for the first time;
red, bulbous, sweating;
a pure thick-necked prick from out past Gort,
and he's wearing one of those black
Thinsulate caps, like you'd pick up
in a petrol station bargain basket-bucket,
so a brand-new van and the auld fucker
wouldn't even buy himself a proper fucking hat,
I mean that's what you're dealing with here,
and he lets off a snarl at you like a tumour
prolapsing out of a badger's arse:

come on to fuck ye're late. I told ye be up by the hotel.

Well by Christ you know what way it's going now,
you have his jib well and truly cut alright,

but you've been out of the scratcher over an hour
and you think you should at least get paid *something*,
anything, stop the whole morning being a total meowl,
a pure woejus altogether,

so you walk around to the passenger door
and open it up. And what drops out?

A rolled-up marquee wall.
Hits you right on the knee.

Put back that fucking wall and get in the back, says he.

**Do you get into the van with the young lad
or do you go back to your own car and drive
home?**

To get in the van, please turn to page 17.

**To get back in your own car and drive home,
please turn to page 14.**

Eight Algorithms For The Self-Driving Self

1. You are driving on a residential street when you are forced to swerve to avoid a van. To your left is a murderer. To your right is a baby.

2. You are travelling through a 50 kmph zone when you are forced to swerve to avoid a truck. To your left is a baby – who will grow up to become an estate agent. To your right are two babies – eating a murderer.

3. You are a zipping along a country lane when you are forced to swerve to avoid a small mountain's solitude. To your left is a text you sent in your twenties. To your right is the one you never could.

4. You are cruising along a motorway when you are forced to swerve to avoid a recently reclassified planet's sense of inadequacy. To your left is a culturally appropriated indigenous votive taking advantage of its now enhanced public profile to exploit lesser and more impressionable effigies. To your right is a Twitterstorm marinating an avocado in beard oil.

5. You are blaring down the Autobahn when you are forced to swerve to avoid the hours invested in the second season of a box-set where the monks break *back in* to the monastery. To your left are the gargoyled eyes of a final year PhD student who's been asked, but in passing, about her thesis. To your right is a national treasure avoiding tax by fly-tipping a paedophile wearing a poppy.

6. You are careening up (and down, simultaneously) a Penrose staircase when you are forced to swerve to avoid the nights you turned down sex to play the computer. To your left is a marmot still maintaining it voted Brexit to make immigration fairer for non-Europeans. To your right is an echidna espousing literal, but à la carte, adherence to scripture.

7. You are hurtling across a Möbius strip when you are forced to swerve to avoid a monocle wearing a Che Guevara t-shirt. To your left is a burning tower block justifying austerity by conflating national expenditure with a household budget (overlooking, of course, that national expenditure raises revenue in a way domestic spending never can). To your right is a woman who CC'd in your line manager.

8. You are flashing between inter-dimensional wormholes when you are forced to swerve to avoid the difference between popularity and populism. To your left is the entirety of your future contained in the eyeballs of a god. To your right is the entirety of your god contained in your future eyeballs.

Hard luck, you have not survived the day with Slab Head.

But you do make it home without further event and get back into bed. You fall asleep and dream so deep that your brain slowly empties.

To play again, return to page 1.
To finish playing, close this book.

The Erection Specialists 2

And more fools the two of you
because that's just what you do.

Turns out the fucking toffee-pockets
has the marquee canvases piled in the front seat
because he's put all the hardware in the back ~
all the aluminium for the frame and the steel footplates
and the fixing pins and the pegs ~

(oh the fucking pegs
oh good *Jee*sus the fucking pegs)

so the back of the van is full of plates and pegs
and apexes and sledgehammers
(actually sledgehammer, singular)
the whole back of the fucking van
filled with every bit of sharpened metal shite
you could think of (but he still only brought
the one hammer because you're not counting
the plastic-headed mallet for tapping down
the floorboards) so, of course, he doesn't want to put
the canvases in the back with all *that;*
just in case a loose Stanley blade or a self-tapper
rips a gouge in a wall ~ or worse,
in a roof ~ well you know that'd cost him see,
because the roofs are all special made in Germany,
they have to be specially fireproofed
and they have these thick nylon seams
that need feeding into the eye-channels on the roof

beams, so that once the marquee frame is standing
the roof can be hauled over the purlins
from the far side by ropes clipped onto the toggles
with carabiners, and if they're out by even a

                              few mils
they won't pull at all (you've made a shite
of your hands before trying to pull a four-metre   roof
that some gowl fed into a twelve-foot bay) so, basically,
no one trusts anyone to make them right
only the Germans, who else but the bloody

                              Germans,

and you know what the slab-headed prick
should have done is pay a joiner to fit out
the back of the van, fit it out properly,
with lidded-boxes to put the canvases in
and separate trays to keep all the small stuff,
all the bolts and the butterfly washers and the spring-pins,

but he was too cheap,

so now the canvases are in the front
and all the metal is just fucked in loose in the back

(even the fucking screws! Not even in a white   plastic
mayonnaise bucket)

so that's why the canvases are piled so high
in the front he can barely see out the window

and why you and the young lad are sitting in the back
perched up on a screed of aluminium
so that every time he brakes the van you get a belt
of a bolt or the hook of a purlin jams sharp
up your hole.

Do you stay in the van or get out at the next traffic lights to ring your partner for a lift home?

To stay in the van, turn to page 22.

To get out at the next traffic lights to ring your partner, turn to page 20.

The Fucking Fuckers

You and J are fucking. Although J is on top of you, neither you nor J think that you are the ones *being* fucked (that is, both of you see yourselves as the *fucker* and neither of you see yourselves as the *fuckee*; and that is both of you see yourselves as doing the fucking and neither as receiving it).

It's not that either of you consider yourselves unequal participants; it's more that in order to see yourselves as *any type* of participant in your fucking you would both require a much more analytical sense of mid-fuck scrutiny than either of you two fucking fuckers can care right now to give.

For you, the view of yourself as the fucker is predominately because it has simply never occurred to you that you might not be one; that is, that you might be a *fuckee*, one who *receives* the fucking? No, this is inconceivable. It would be like trying to understand blindness by closing your eyes instead of by studying a picture through your elbow.

For J, however, it is different. J is not above thinking of themselves as a *fuckee* on occasion (and here J is more honest than you, because J will admit to, in the past, having been happily most happily fucked). But J refuses to accept that whether choosing – yes, *choosing* – to become a *fuckee* is determined by anything so arbitrary as mere position. What about when you are both lying on your sides? Or both standing up? Or both draped over a chair like wet coats? Clearly, mere position does not always help discern who it is that's doing the fucking and to whom, and thus what determines someone's status as a *fucker* or a *fuckee* must be something else and, yes, while it's true that, right now and lying on your back, you are being more thrust upon than thrusting, but *you know* it was in fact J who instigated this particular fuck by turning your skin as sharp as bark with a careful brush of a hand and so, if – *if!* – J is now *choosing* to be a fuckee then it is only because J has acquiesced: and acquiescence is born from choice and choice is born from power, and power means, of course, that in J choosing to *not own* the fucking it is in fact J who owns it after all.

So, when J comes with a wet clench and collapses on you like an ironing board, You are tempted – *almost* tempted – to say 'That was so good'.

But you don't – knowing, of course, that saying 'that was *so* good' is really saying: 'please reassure me that you enjoyed that to at least something approaching a similar level as I did and that we are at least on an equivalent plane of fucking and that I am not in a river while you are, say, in a puddle'.

So you don't say anything. But then J rolls over and says, 'That was *so* good'.

You sleep in fitful snatches after that, shallow dreams that break like poppadums, until you find yourself awake once more. The moon is coming in through the curtain, landing on J's face so it's unclear whether J is smiling or dreaming of finding loose change. You pause – then shuffle into J, lick an earlobe, trace down J's thigh with a fingernail. J stirs awake and you whisper through the darkness *fuck me, fuck me hard'*, your words ringing out like a klaxon opening a Black Friday sale.

Hard luck, you have not survived the day with Slab Head.

J gets up and has a shower. You stay in bed and sniff your fingers.

To play again, return to page 1. To finish playing, close this book.

The Erection Specialist 3

Have you ever sat in the back of a Mercedes
Sprinter on two ton of untethered metal
from Salthill to Letterfrack?

Every fucking lump,
every fucking bump

(and there's some amount of both
once you get out of Spiddal,
because he didn't go
direct on the N59, of course,
and just to spite you)

and unless you get your hands up
quick all the metal lifts up off the van
floor and you with it
and you cop a clatter of the roof on the head
before all the aluminium comes smacking
back down with a sickening rattle,
throwing up clouds of dust that tastes
like a nosebleed, not that you can see this though,
because it's pitch black,
pitch black save one chink of light slicing
up from the footwell

(the same footwell
where the young lad ends up
twice in a tangled heap when Slab Head slams
on the brakes)

and the ear-battering noise,
every pebble and flake of a stone
shooting up against the wheel arches,
all the bars and the poles, shaking,
shaking until your ears are whining
violence through the dark
and that's how it went,
the whole way out past Letterfrack
right until the soft and merciful cringle
of the van rolling slow over loose chippings

(chickens I used to think it was,
on the road signs when I heard it
as a child, *beware of loose chickens* ~
can you imagine?).

The engine cuts and you hear him get out
and you're waiting,
but even though you're both gone feral
from being in the back you still don't
want the van door to slide open
with its metal cough signalling
a day's work clearing its throat
because you know then
you'll both have to get out
and start pigging around two tons of aluminium.

But the door opens.

Do you stay in the van to dream of happier times or get out and start working?

To stay in the van and dream of happier times, turn to page 24.

To get out and start working, turn to page 26.

How The Grass Got In

That summer it was a beehive;
that summer it was a flume;
that summer it was a jut-nail
on the wall of a full cloakroom.

That summer was a mangrove
and half the crabs below,
that summer was the sock you lost
by the gurning of the Sergeant's brow.

That summer was every whirling hem
in a pre-war Viennese ball,
and you were but one lacquered plank
feasting on each light footfall,

that summer was twenty labouring men
stood fast in brawny boots,
and you were the ways they tried fright-by the days
with their bawdy hollers and whoops.

That summer was a Punjab pirate
(complete with swarthy entourage)
and you were but its shaking fist
as it damned the evil Raj,

that summer huffed-up half your windows
and drew on your breath-wet glass,
then pried loose half your skirting boards
'til in flew the wild ryegrass.

Hard luck, you have not survived the day with Slab Head.

After extensive roaring and shouting, Slab Head gives up. When the coast is clear, you get out of the van and spend the next eight hours in the first pub you find.

To play again, return to page 1.

To finish playing, close this book.

The Erection Specialist 4

Even though it's mizzle-grey outside
you're still blinded from being in the dark so long,
and you slither over the aluminium
and unfurl yourself like a snail's eye.

You are in the corner of a basketball court,
the cracked asphalt playground
of a small and white-washed primary school,
and you can tell the young lad is thinking the same as you,
which is this: where the fuck was the forklift.

Because no forklift means lifting the entire marquee
frame up by hand, all twenty fucking
bays of it, and it's Röder gear we're talking here,
the stuff with the real heavy fixings,

but before you can think about it too much more
auld Slab Head is off on one, effing and bloody blinding,

get that fucking stuff out of the back of the van

but he hasn't told you where anything is going

not there you fucking apes

now *you* know the best way to do it
is to lay everything out where it needs to go,
instead of double-handling it all
by *first* fucking it out of the van into one random pile

and *then* having to sort *that* fucking random pile out all
over again
by moving everything to where it actually should've gone
in the first fucking place

there, over there you pair of thicks

oh by fuck there's nothing worse
than double-handling on a day-rate

Here! Put that fucking apex here!

and he has you on a day-rate right enough.

His eyes are now ayting into you as you work,
And even simple things
like carrying a poxy wall-bar
and you're gone all fumbled
and so come two hours later you've only done one
hour's work.

Slab Head is really bulling now.
He marches over, grabs you hard on the arm.

Is there anything you can *fucking do?* he says.

You nod.

Well can you square a fucking tent?

And you nod again,
because you can,
you've done it many a time.

27

He stomps off to the van and fucks you out
two tape measures from the front seat.

Squared and pegged by the time I get back, he says.

and then he drives off
to fuck knows where.

**Do you keep working or do you fuck off home
and read the paper?**

To keep working, turn to page 30.

**To fuck off home and read the paper, turn to
page 29.**

Suspicion

You are sitting in the garden.
The paper is in the new Berliner format.
There is a single bee
in-and-out the clematis
and half a sugar in your coffee.

A headline says:

SUSPECTED IMMIGRANTS FOUND DEAD
IN LORRY

It's finally happened, you think.

You can be suspected
of being an immigrant now.

**Hard luck, you have not survived the day.
With Slab Head.**

**While reading the paper, despondency runs
through you like a jolt through a rope. It
passes, and you close the paper and scroll
through Facebook.**

To play again, return to page 1.
To finish playing, close this book.

The Erection Specialist 5

With him gone it's almost pleasant.

The mizzle starts lifting and you see
you're on the coast, right by a sweeping
beach where the sea looks like you
can walk out a mile and still only be up to your
shins,and the breeze is fresh, and you start showing
the young lad how to square the marquee.

You show him how to set out the first footplate

(by hammering a peg into the ground
and then tying an orange string-line
to the peg and running the line off down the side)

then how to lay out the next footplate
parallel to the string-line

(making sure there's exactly
five metres between it and the first)

and then how to lay out the third, the tricky one,
by laying it twenty feet across from the first plate
and squaring it off by using the two measuring tapes
to form a 3~4~5 triangle

(but ensuring, of course, that the young lad
is holding the zero ends of both tapes)

and then how to at last lay out the rest of the plates

(still measuring five metres from centre-fixing
to centre-fixing)

before driving in the pegs, four into each,
so the metal fuckers can't move an inch.

Now when you say 'pegs' you don't mean
thin bits of wire for a festival tent,
no you're talking iron pegs here,
two-and-a-half foot long,
each with a tread cut into the length of the shaft
so they bite into the ground, big thick
iron spikes with wide heads so you can really
burst them with the sledge,
and you start grabbing them up from the rusty
pile on the tarmac

and as you lay them out they seem to you
to come from every genus and family of marquee
peg in the world; some have diamond heads
and some have wide, round heads like huge thumb-tacks,
and others have square heads with a nub in the centre,
and some even have patterns on the shafts,
spirals or raffia effects etched into them,

(and who is it that spends time cutting ornate patterns
into a lump of iron whose sole purpose in this world
is to be battered to shite by a sledgehammer?

Now that there is a quare kind of love indeed,
and maybe if we had even *a quarter*
of that kind of love for each other
then the world might be even an eighth alright,
and, anyway, where and why and how
in the name of Jeesus had Slab Head gathered

himself such a far-flung collection?
Like he was some demented pirate
of the seven seas of tent-mongery?
And that there indeed was an odd love inside of him
too, though none of it left for you
or anything else not made of metal).

But by fuck it's the pegs where the problems start.
All eighty-four of the big iron bastards.

First up, that insufferable and slab-headed prick
has left you with only one sledge. Here you are,
both on a day-rate, and eighty-four fucking pegs
to drive before you can stop for lunch
but with only the one sledge between you ~
and even that is only a gammy yoke,
the head has been fixed on the cheap,
by driving down a small wedge of wood
in-between the hole in the lump and the top
of the handle to try stop the fourteen-pound metal head
flying off when you swing it

(you hope).

But worse it gets.
The first peg sinks down a foot or so easy
enough, just two solids smacks with the sledge,

the tarmac is old and soft as pudding
so the peg punches right through it,
down through the compacted layers of hardcourt
and you think it's going to be a handy one ~
but then nothing.

Nothing frigging nothing.
Not a budge not a peep not a scridgen.
You both taking turns to burst the peg
with all your might but it's shifting only a few
mils each time and the reverberations are kicking
back up the hammer and right up your arm,
rattling your shoulder sharper than a cat's cock,
the ball going to jump clean out of the socket,
and it turns out the whole playground is sitting
on a bed of solid rock, some huge lump of cunting
Connemerara schist or quartzite,
and the line of fat crows nesting on the mossy
school roof are sending their caws clattering down
through your ears, to hell or to Connaught they say
but both mean the same thing to you.

No; *you* know what that tight prick *should* have done
is paid for a ground survey; then he'd have known
to bring a pneumatic hammer

(or better, two pneumatic hammers.
Or better still a forklift.
Because you've driven down pegs
with a three-wheeled Moffet before,
lined it up just right and dropped the forks

with a tap of the paddle. And how can a man
who runs a marquee company not have a forklift
anyways? But that, right there,
is all the love he bears you).

But every peg the same,
every single one,
and because they aren't going *down* when you hit them
they move to the *side* instead,

33

widening out the hard one holes you've made
and then falling off at an angle
so hammering them straight becomes impossible,
and you have to take turns holding
the shafts for each other,
crouching down,
one hand grasping the peg,
as low as you can
your head held back as far as possible,
holding tight to the rusty iron
and staring at your foot
trying to ignore the huge and arcing lump
of the sledge cracking down on the peg-head,
the sparks kicking off it,
the metallic whine ringing out
like a Godzilla raping a hole in a cyborg,
and if the young lad misses
or the wobbly head comes off
then that's it,
arm broke,
worse,
lying on the ground
with a head like a pulped fig

(and it's a long way from a hospital you are now).

**The imminent fear of death reminds you of a
funeral that's happening today.**

Do you keep working or do you go to the funeral?

To keep working, turn to page 37.

To go to the funeral, turn to page 35.

The Rasher Bolya

You heard The Rasher died stitched to his britches.
You heard that, the night he died, roads spluttered up sharp
slabs and then a crowd came down, as quick and black as flies.
Their dirge was the low moan of gravity getting rimmed.

You heard that the town had gargled The Rasher too saltily,
that the men had loved him for the women who loved him
and the women had loved him for the love of these men.
You heard he'd made the factories tick like glockenspiels,

that root vegetables grew up in his footsteps, that a housewife
exploded watching him whistle and so her son then hung
long white wreathes from his ears. You heard the town's tears
fell like an angels' ejaculate, each drop more painful

than lipstick on a child. You heard that The Rasher
dreamt like a dervish, that he sang like a stone, was really

more mackerel than man. You heard a priest once cast his face
in Formica, transubstantiated it in the tabernacle and out

came a crow, you heard his funeral crawled the streets
like Parkinson's down a surgeon's arm, that as The Rasher
was lowered tongue-like into the empty socket of his grave
the howl loosed shook whole families from their trees

and the church bells rang out like a blowjob on a ruby
anniversary. You heard what you heard.

You know, of course, that the town can never be the same.
But maybe, and with help, you heard one day it might try.

Hard luck, you have not survived the day with Slab Head.

But Rasher's wake is mighty and free drink flows like free drink at a mighty wake.

To play again, return to page 1.
To finish playing, close this book.

The Erection Specialist 6

So that's how you spend all morning
and half the afternoon,
alternating between shitting yourself inside-out
for fear of losing your fingers
and then flashing your arms arthritic
by hammering iron spikes into what
might as well be concrete.

Fat, dark blood-blisters well up
On your hands, like grapes, and you strip
to your waist, eyes stinging, sweat dripping
from your nose, salt caking the slopes
of your cheeks, working so hard you smoke
entire fags in your mouth as you swing
the hammer, the ear-splitting rings drowning
out the laughter of the fat feathery fuck-hounds
perched up on the lichened roof behind,
each peg going down

a millimetre
a millimetre
a millimetre
at a time

but you get it done

by fuck you get it done

at it since eight
and now nearing two o'clock
but every fucking peg sunk down
at last all the pegs bet
finally, finally bet.

You fall on the ground, caked in sweat
and dust. You've barely stopped, only for a skull
of water or to cup a palmful to your face,
the back of your neck,
and the young lad pulls his sandwich
out of a plastic Dunnes bag ~
and then you realise

that Slab Head is after driving off

with your bollixing lunch box.

Do you stay around in the hope of bumming some food off the young lad or do you give up on this day altogether and start another one?

To stay around in the hope of bumming some food of the young lad, turn to page 41.

To give up on this day altogether and start another one, turn to page 39.

The Fun House

You spent the night in the bath.
Miroslav pours you into it,
dragging you face-down 'cross the carpet
when your snoring saws through

even his black-stilts of sleep.
The next morning you learn some things:
whole pylons can be sunk in the depths
of a foreman's fury, how it is a day becomes

the week, the true weight of two ton of timber.
At lunchtime your box is empty.
Jonty laughs at you, you eye his sandwich.
'You're useless today,' he says,

'we'd be better off traipsing the timbers
with a jellyfish'. 'Miroslav used to be a body builder,'
you say. 'Whose bloody body was he building?'
says Koresh and sighs, before breaking you

off half his soft egg-roll. Jonty has a gold earring,
can lift a whole fence panel over his head
with one hand, pretends to send money home
to his wife. The pretence is for you, his wife knows.

Koresh has eyes that flick like whips.
You hear, later, that he's inside now for opening
an artery with a pin pulled loose from a bumper car.
That afternoon you screw a thousand brittle little bulbs

into the mouths of painted clowns on the House of Fun.
That afternoon you learn some more things:
that when you've slept in a bath you sure conduct a current,
that Miroslav likes pottery, that Koresh has never met
his children, that sometimes you are a villain
but mostly you are like electricity,
just seeking the path of least resistance.

Hard luck, you have not survived the day with Slab Head.

But the rest of your life is pleasant, if unspectacular. Some years later you bump into Jonty again in a supermarket and have a conversation about turmeric.

To start again, return to page 3.
To finish playing, close this book.

The Erection Specialist 7

The poor young lad doesn't know what to do.

The day's work you've just put in
and he's only desperate to horse into his sanger,
to drink off his creamy pint
of milk ~ but fair play because he breaks
you off a bit (doesn't make too much effort
to get the ham though, when it won't tear) and he pours
out a glunk of milk into your empty water bottle
and you sit there without speaking,
chewing,
looking at the tent you've squared,
at the eighty-three pegs you've bet,

looking out further beyond;
to the haze over the Connemara coast
to the sparkling of the afternoon sun on the sea,

and you start to think:

do you know what?
do you know what?
this isn't that bad,
yeah some days are better than others
but when you weigh it all up
there are worst places to be,
you could be stuck in an office all day
or be out there on one of those poxy boats
scrounging for a few fish

The breeze blows in on you,
it's fresh and wet and the sun
is warm, perfect for tanning,
you feel yourself browning like a nut
as you sit there.

You check your phone.
Only been stopped fifteen minutes
so you turn to the young lad:

come on, you say
come on and we'll go for a swim.

And he looks at you,
the big daft bastard,

and cracks out his first smile
of the whole bloody day.

Do you go swimming or go get a different job?

To go swimming, turn to page 46.

To get a different job, turn to page 43.

Burger Foods

You're cleaning the freezer again. It's dark, apart from that one bulb in the ceiling covered by the blue plastic casing and a metal grill. The light in the freezer is a pale blue, the same ghosty colour of the lights in the public toilets to stop smack heads finding a vein. You can't imagine there's a problem with people shooting up in the cold-store of an unnamed and totally fictional fast food chain – but you get an image of moving a stack of frozen Whoppers and discovering a cryogenic junkie with a belt still on his bicep. The thought makes you step backwards into a box of fries and you end up with your arse planted into a tray of cold meat patties. Icy bits of burger soak down your pants and up your hole. *Frozen flame grilled cunts,* you say. You're about to stand up – but decide against it. There's nothing actually needs to be cleaned in here. The freezer is, in fact, spotless – and you know it's spotless because you cleaned it yesterday (and the day before). You're only in the freezer because your manager sends you in out of pure spite, spite because you refuse to clock-out when it's quiet and go sit in the staffroom so that you're not getting paid. It's one of her strategies to keep the costs on her shifts down – however, you know (after some research) that's it's illegal and so you refuse to do it. Now, in a bid to break you, whenever you refuse to clock-out she makes you first scrub the abominably grease-soaked grill hoods and then go in to clean the freezer so all the manky burger grease solidifies into your hair. Your manager is not used to people refusing to clock-out. Most of the other people who

43

work the night shifts with you are Chinese students who, legally, can only work 19 hours a week – but your manager allows them to register using both their English names AND their Chinese names, so now they can work 38 hours because they show up as two separate people on the wage slips so they are too scared to refuse her cost-cutting overtures. But, even though you've tried hate her for all this, you can't. You've seen her crying in the office when she needs to fill in the weekly target charts, and you still remember how the man from headquarters got up in her face; shouting so loudly about her excessive use of cheese in the quarter-pounders with cheese (*use lettuce instead! Lettuce is cheap – cheese is not!*) that he left spittle all over her glasses. After ten more minutes watching your breath clump in the blue air you reach the maximum amount of time Health and Safety says a person can spend in a freezer, so you get up and leave. Your manager is hiding in the office pretending to do something with spreadsheets, and the next few hours pass uneventful; save for an argument with a customer who waves a gerkin at you and shouts *I told you no cucumbers!* (in the end turns out you were both right) and another customer who has eaten all but the final crumb of her burger but is now at the counter complaining the mayonnaise was off and thus demanding another burger full of the very same mayonnaise in recompense. When it's time for your *actual* break, you do clock-out and go to sit in staff room with a bag of onion rings. Roy is already there, noisily drinking a milkshake, and you sit across from him on a blue plastic chair which is fixed to the floor. *Is Roy a popular name in China?* you ask him and he laughs, before telling you his Chinese name (which he correctly predicts you won't be able to pronounce). He then tells you he went to the cinema at the weekend.

What did you see? you ask him. *The Passions of Christ*, he says. *Did you like it?* you say. *It was O.K*, he says, *but I didn't understand the story – who was the main character? And why did no one like him and why was he carrying the big stick?* Your manager is still crying into the recalcitrant rows of her spreadsheets and you know you've now got thirteen minutes to explain the whole concept of Jesus to a notional Buddhist who speaks only conversational English. *Right*, you say to Roy offering him an onion ring, *you see there was this donkey, right – no, forget the donkey, there was this star – no, no, actually, there was a king doing a census – What's a census?* he says. *Ah, here, jaysus – look*, you say handing him over an onion ring, *you're going to need another one of these—*

Hard luck, you have not survived the day. And it seems this job may, in fact, be even worse than the one you left.

To play again, return to page 1.

To finish playing, close this book.

The Erection Specialist 8

The sea is deeper than you thought.

You are up to your waist soon enough
and it's cold, but it is great to feel
layers of dirt lift off you like clingwrap,
to take a deep breath and duck your head
under, to feel your chest shrink like some
huge claw is grabbing you, and then to burst

up, shake your head,
the grey dust-slime
slide out from your nose.

When you're finished, you sit on the beach,
free of the casings of your boots
and your toes buried in the coolness of the sand,
the breeze softly flaying you,
and you watch the little clippers crawl
silent over the horizon while you root
your last two fags out from the side-pocket

of your Snickers trousers. You give one
to the young lad, crinkle up the empty
box and spark up.

Why do you think he's such a cunt? you say,
lean back on an elbow.
The young lad stiffens,
the knobbled curve of his spine disappearing
off into his back

and you know he has something for you then,
something worth listening to,
and he turns to you, a look on his face
like his brain is sliding around tiles inside
to unscramble a picture.

He wasn't always such a prick,
he says, lighting his fag.

I worked for him a few years back,
he was flying it then, thirty people under him
five just in the yard, but a lad from Donegal,
Decky I think his name was, started
and Syl asked him
to drill a few drainage holes in a steel gutter ~

~ the tide had come in and you leaned forward
to save your boots getting wet
from a charge of water rolling up the beach ~

but your man Decky was too lazy
to go get the drill battery so he decided
to use a nail and a lump hammer.
But sure the first whack he hit, didn't the nail
just fly off, and the hammer bounced back up
because of the spring in the steel
and planted him square in the face

~ he stops to smoke his fag ~

knocked out six of his teeth.
And then he got in such a rage
that he fucked the hammer
clean through the windscreen of Syl's van.

What did Syl do? you say.

Sacked him.
On the spot.
But sure then didn't Decky go
and sue him for twenty grand?

You let off a low whistle
and the young lad nods.

And Syl had a few other things like that too.
Another lad he hired took a shite
in the corner of a wedding marquee
and the bride's mother stepped right in it.
Syl had to give them twenty grand too.
And one time some other fella went AWOL
and Syl found him having a wank
on a pile of silk lining bags.
And then the recession came,
contractors stopped paying him,
and sure no one had money for marquees
* anymore anyhow, so Syl*
had to sell everything, even the forklifts.
So now Syl thinks we're all just out to fuck
him and so he's decided to fuck us all first.

Why are you back with him? you say.

The young lad gives you a second goofy smile.

Me and a mate are over to Perth next week,
out of this shit-hole, going working in the mines.
So I need a few bob, and Syl always pays on time,
even when he was gone to the wall
he was always straight with the wages.

Well he's still a miserable prick, you say.

Yea, the young lad says, *but wouldn't you be a miserable prick too?*

The little trawlers are still crawling far out on the water
and the sky is now cloudless
the colour of the memory of a summer
and your skin has gone taught from the salt
left by the evaporating sea
and the bit of the sandwich is sitting nice in your stomach
and you take your phone out of your pocket

quarter to three

Erection Specialists? you say, well come on then
Crocodile Dundee, let's go and get this marquee finished
for the poor miserable bastard.

And the young lad smiles for the third time.
and you get up and walk back to the school yard
swinging your boots in our hands as you go
so your toes can enjoy their last minutes of freedom.

**Do you go back to work or lie on the beach
and reminisce?**

To go back to work, turn to page 51.

**To lie on the beach and reminisce, turn to
page 50.**

The Mongrel

The mongrel has been stalking you of late.

It appears in the most unexpected places;
the storeroom of your Saturday job,
out cutting the grass, while watching
Murder She Wrote. You even heard it one afternoon
growling out from a patch of conifers.

This morning it followed you to school again.
Old Man Flanagan was scribing the pluperfect
on the board in his looping letters when you realise
it has snuck inside, is now under your desk
and nubbling between your thighs with a wet pink
nose. *Shush* you say, sit as still as pilchards
hoping it will turn a few short circles,
go to sleep
but it starts a gentle yapping,
twitchings like slivers of fish flashing through
a pond. Then comes a drooling from its chops
and you know a full-scale barking is on the way.
You ask for the bathroom.

Sat on the cold porcelain of a school toilet
you finally let it loose, let it lick your fingers
with its angry purple breath. You stroke it,
tickle it in under the chin as you try calm it down
amid the silver bells of all the filling cisterns.

**Hard luck, you have not survived the day.
Your mind is full, your pockets are empty**

To play again, return to page 1.

To finish playing, close this book.

The Erection Specialist 9

When you climb back over the low wall
into the yard you see the van is back,
and hitched to the back,
with the front wheels up on the tow trolley,
is an orange forklift.

It's a small one, a Toyota you reckon,
more suited for shunting pallets around
a warehouse, but you can see the gas cylinder
on the back just over the counterweight block

that'll do, you think,
that'll lift the frame up just fine,
and you turn and hit the young lad
a playful dig in the arm
we'll be home for dinner yet.

But as you cross the yard,
boots still in your hands,
Syl appears from the back of the van
(and still wearing that bloody fucking hat)
and stalks across the asphalt
like he's just caught you pissing in his garden.
He starts really effing and blinding now,
worse than ever,
and waving a claw hammer high over his head

I'm not paying youse two to go fucking paddling,
youse fucking lazy cunts

and you look around at the work you've done,
the eighty pegs you've driven
into the cunting Connemara earth
with only one poxy sledge

It's because of lazy fuckers like ye I'm gone broke

and you see the sweat left on each of them
and then the waiting around Salthill for an hour
in the grey rain, and your lunch that's still in the van

your poor lovely sandwich, how you'd got up at five
just to make it so that you didn't have to make it the
night before because then it would be soggy by the morning
but now it was gone all soggy anayway, all sour and
soggy and shite

because of lazy good-for-nothing hoors like ye

and after all that here's Syl, still coming towards you,
still roaring and bawling,
waving a hammer, calling you a lazy gouger cunt

and you lose it, lose it
and you whirl a boot by the laces
swing it round in a vicious loop

and by Christ do you let it fly

watch it spiral through the air

toe over heel

heel over toe

spinning straight for Syl's face

and then you watch

Syl bob his big slab of a head

and the steel toecap go whizzing past

without leaving a mark.

By now you've reached the marquee
but he's still coming at you,
face purpled in rage, hammer cocked
in violence over his shoulder,
and you bend down
and pull up the peg you'd used to run off the string-line
and you're thinking:

ah fuck it
ah here it is now
ah Christ you're going to have to brain this bastard
going to end up doing life in the Joy
all because Decky from Donegal
couldn't be arsed to use a drill

and he's right on you now,
hammer raised even higher
and you spin back,
put your chin over your left shoulder,

twist your hips and coil your stomach,
and then

lash the fucking peg around
at the full length of your arm

feel it gather its terrible and pendulous momentum

and you spin your head back round

just in time to see

that the fucking young lad

the stupid fucking young lad

has come around from your right
to try make a grab for Syl's hammer

but Syl has ducked again,
his head, celestial big yet you can't ever hit it,
and you watch in silence
as the pointed end of the peg
sails right over the hunch of Syl's shoulders
and catches the young lad
flush in the face

with a wet slop
like a dollop of mortar
being dropped on a trowel

his fourth and final smile of the day
the one you carve into his face
with the sharp end of that patterned iron spike.

It's late the next evening
when the ferry leaves Belfast
and it's near two weeks later again
when you pick up the Indo
in a greasy pub in Perth
to read what you already knew:

that Yvonne Murtagh's youngest son
is buried in the hard Connemara ground
all because some fella you never met
took a shite in the corner of a wedding tent.

Congratulations!

You have now survived the full day (unlike the young lad Murtagh) and Slab Head pays you a fair day's wages.

To play again, turn to page 1.

To finish playing, close this book.

Acknowledgements

The Erection Specialist (parts 1-9) were first published together as a short story called *The Erection Specialist* by The Honest Ulsterman. The poem *Eight Algorithms For The Self Driving Self* was first published on the University of Royal Holloway website.

To begin laying out your unrest,
write a poem

To finish laying out your unrest,
edit the poem

www.ingramcontent.com/pod-product-compliance
Lightning Source LLC
Chambersburg PA
CBHW021942040426
42448CB00008B/1202